AQÜITÍN

ENVIRONMENTAL EDUCATIVE MAGAZINE

OF WATER AND NATURE FOR CHILDREN

No 1

AUTHOR: Lic Yolanda Ma Jorge Besteiro
TRANSLATER: Lic José M. Ramos Hernández
Lic   Yolanda F. Rodríguez Toledo

Index of Sections and Topics:

Section 1: Why the name water? Distribution of water on the planet.

Section 2. Recommendation on how to dispose of used household oil.

Section 3 Story about the life of Aqüitín.

Section 4. Story "Alba the Blue Whale"

Section 5. Learn what the hydrological cycle is.

Section 6. "Natural" crossword

Section 7. Vocabulary and concepts of natural phenomena.

Section 8. Stay up-to-date with the news for the children and youth of the family.

Section 9 Contest call.

Water is a common good for all.

Section 1

Curiosities about the planet earth. "Did you know...?

Water (from the Latin aqua) is a substance composed of one atom of oxygen and two of hydrogen. At room temperature it is liquid, odorless, tasteless and colorless, although it acquires a slight blue hue in large volumes. It is fundamental for the existence of life. No life form is known to occur in the complete absence of this molecule.

Water is distributed on the planet in an irregular way, with the largest amount of it in a salty form. No less than 97% is salty and is found in the seas and oceans. Only 3% of the water is fresh. 79% of this 3% is frozen forming the polar caps and glaciers.

The above data expressed in percent when representing them in volumes of water, we can say that: the total volume of water on earth is 1,400 million km3, a volume consisting of 97% of salt water:
Of the 39 million fresh water available, only 10 million km3 of water is usable (the other part is in the form of ice).

Did you know that ... The renewal fees of the water, or mean residence time, in each of the phases of the hydrological cycle are not the same. For example, the water in the oceans is slowly renewed, once every 3,000 years, while atmospheric vapor does so rapidly, approximately every 10 days.

This means that the same water that existed millions of years ago on Earth is still the same. Thanks to the water cycle, the same water is continually being recycled around the world.

It is perfectly probable that the water you drink in the morning was once used by a prehistoric animal.

Yes like that, make no mistake about it, of course it was fresh water, Aqüitín tells you, who knows a lot about water.

Oceans of the world.

According to astronauts 35,000 km away, our planet certainly looks like the planet of water because of the large surface area they occupy and this water is distributed in three large ocean basins, which have an average depth of 3.8 km.

Although it can be considered that there is only one world ocean that communicates with the rest, for the study of these, the marine hydrosphere is divided into three large oceans: the Pacific, the Atlantic and the Indian, and a series of adjacent seas. A recent trend assigns also to the Antarctic waters the category of ocean.

-Did you know what ... If the salt content (Sodium Chloride) could be extracted from all the world's oceans, with this salt we could cover all the continents up to a height of 1.5 meters? Incredible no!

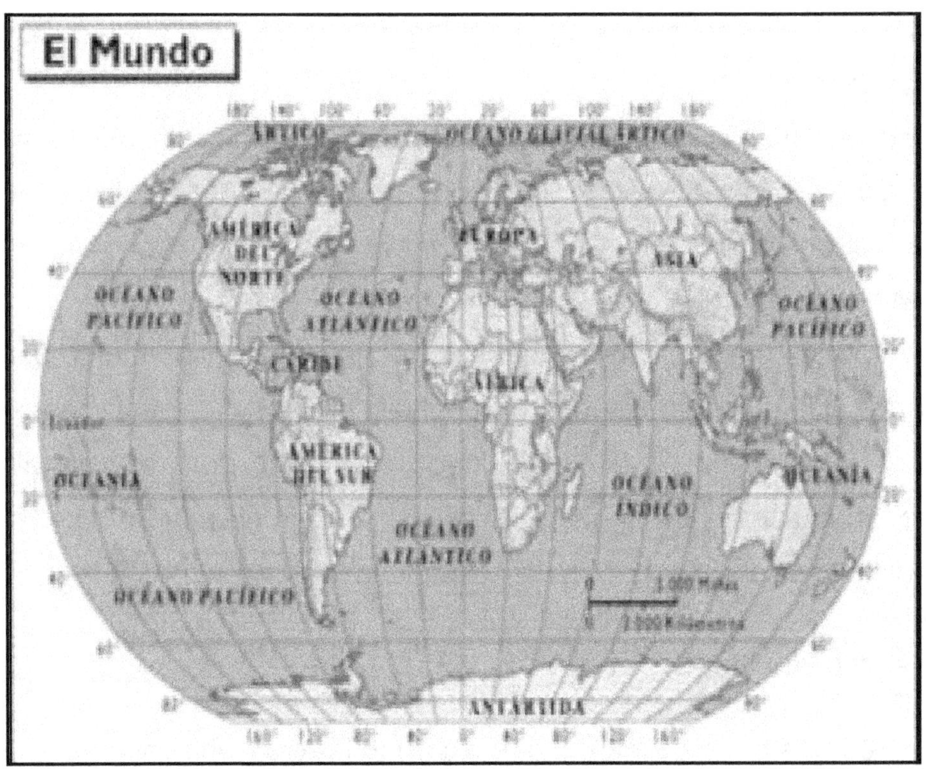

Section 2 Recommendations. "Do the best for everyone"

You will agree with Aquitín that we must do the best for everyone, that is why it is essential to be well informed, for example, at home we must take into account that:

Used oil pollutes the water. That is why it should not be disposed of down the kitchen sink, landfill, or toilet, or in any sink.

This would be terrible, although we often see our mothers doing it this way without thinking about the consequences, often out of ignorance.
Imagine that all that used oil that runs through the landfill joins the waters sewer system and just one liter of oil (1 liter), pollutes about one million liters of water that a person can consume for 14 years.
For this reason, we suggest that you choose the most appropriate way to dispose of used oil, it is easy to do and does not harm anyone, we all win if you choose to do it as we will teach you in our magazine, following the simple steps that we will tell you below:

1-First, you take a plastic bottle.

2-Pour the used oil into it, taking care to leave it well covered.

3-Throw it into the container of plastic containers for household waste.

So, by choosing this simple act of removing the oil in the way we recommend you avoid losing so much water.

You can contribute to the elimination of used oil in this way from the family bosom in which you live and if you tell your classmates, we will be more, those who take care of our water. Water belongs to everyone, **so we must all take care of it**.

Section 3. Story. "Once upon a time"

Before telling you something about the life of Aqüitín we want to invite you to think about all the possible paths that our friend water follows and to draw a picture of your idea about the path of a drop of water that comes out of the sink when you shower and the amount of water you consume in this daily activity.

"The life of Aqüitín"

One morning, on Jacinto's farm where the flowers were watered, there was a precious drop of water lost. It was Aquitín, the poor thing, together with her sisters, was very frightened because she was walking and walking and she didn't even realise it.

Aqüitín, impeccably clean and translucent as crystal, shone on the petals of a beautiful flower. The afternoon sun illuminated it and it seemed as if the rainbow itself gave it its hand and was perched on those petals, beautiful colours formed through the light, making it look like a beautiful spring dragonfly. The droplet was splendid, but her fear did not allow her to enjoy her admirers who sighed in astonishment, even a little butterfly landed there. A whole line of blonde ants, panting from the long way up the stem of the flower, came towards it, which unsuspectingly did not even flinch.

From a sparrow's nest, a very daring and curious little sparrow approached it, drinking tiny particles from it. The droplet had no room for itself, desperation took hold of its will and, trying to propel itself, it slid and plummeted towards a lower branch which offered it a splendid leaf to rest on for a few moments. Suddenly, a gentle breeze blew the drop and carried it away, but not before some of it fell to the ground, which swallowed it up in one bite.

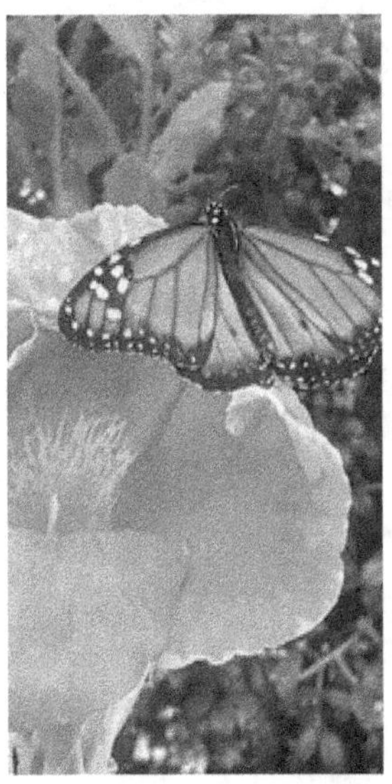

Something similar happened to the tiny particle of the drop that remained on the leaf, it was so hot that the poor thing lost consciousness, it felt like it was floating in the air, rising and rising: when it recovered and opened its eyes it realized that it was in the infinite blue sky, wrapped in a giant cloud that grew bigger and bigger and changed from grey to dark blackish tones. It was then that water began to fall from it in the form of small, fine, transparent drops, perfuming the immeasurable space with scents that only water knows how to leave when it wets the thirsty earth, the grateful plants and the flowers that fan themselves with the fall of the water and the movement of the air.

While many small drops of water were being absorbed by the ground, moving rapidly downwards and sideways, the water felt divided into fractions of multiple drops that were lost in the infinite thirsty earth. Those that ran sideways were attracted by the roots of the plants that covered the ground. The roots became turgid and moist with gratitude, sharing the absorbed water with the rest of the plant, ascending through the stem to the exposed upper parts of the soil surface.

The rest that escaped from the roots reached deep into the infinite depths of the earth, Aqüitín, surprised, felt how in its path tiny channels opened up and became imperceptible pores that she had never believed existed in the depths of the earth. Everything was dark when, without thinking, she began to feel a certain relief and freshness. He had reached a large body of water. He could not believe it.

- Is it possible that I am dreaming, she thought excitedly.

Clear, sweet water! -She shrieked with joy, tasted and looked up but could not see anything, she was already part of the great mass of fresh water that at first seemed static, but after a while and remained very quiet she perceived a slight movement in herself, slipping into the crevices of the ground.

It took tens of thousands of years on its very long journey, but our friend was still intact and as young and transparent as the first day. From where she stood, she perceived that the earth ceased to be earth and turned into stones and later into rocks, from where a gush of water came to the light, impacting against large rocks that ended in a stream.

There in the crystal-clear waters of the stream, the drop watched in bewilderment as the animals grazing on the shore drank the fresh, fresh water.

After a good nap, now calmer and without worries, she felt that the intense heat of the sun overheated the water and she had the sensation of burning on the surface of the water, which burned and smoked, that is what the little drop felt and she believed that she would never be small again, as she felt sheltered and protected in this great mass of water.

What would not be her surprise when she began to feel herself rising and rising through the air and looked down and saw the horses getting smaller and smaller as if those beasts were like round dots that were lost in the spacious earth.

Aqüitín together with other drops was covered in a white cloud, amidst the smoke, forming incredible figures with the passing of the wind.

The water that had been left behind on the ground joined all the water that had fallen from the cloud and in a tightly bound mass the sisters of the water ran and ran across the ground. The birds and all the animals of the field were refreshed in the cool summer rain.

Nearby there is a water well which, while it was raining, stored up a lot of water, which Jacinto then pumped back into the field to water his flowers and also to use in his house.

When he arrives tired from his work, he needs a good bath and his wife has prepared his dinner using the same water he takes from the well.

While all these things happen at the same time, our friend Aqüitín, the funniest of all water drops, rejoices in travelling the different paths she already knows and other new ones that she will tell you about another time.

She will do so throughout her life, time and again she will change forms without getting tired, she will pass from one state to another travelling incredible distances, her life is a sequence of cyclical events that only she "the water" can and has the capacity to follow.

THE END

Section 4. Curiosities about whales.

Alba is a giant whale, men call her the blue whale, they don't call her by her real name, some unknowing people refer to her as the monster of the waters, but she is not. Many fear her because of her great size, but Alba is noble and friendly to her friends.

When she is older, she wants to have a family, she longs to be a mother, to walk her little one across the ocean. Alba measures thirty-two meters and is the heaviest of the creatures that has inhabited the seas.

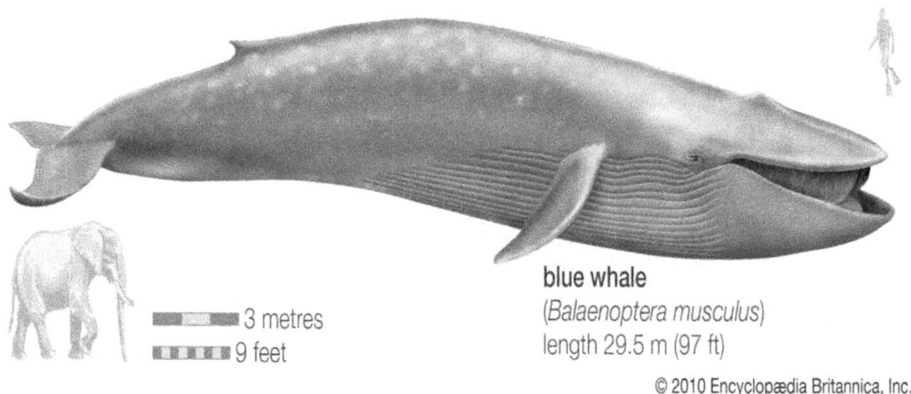

blue whale
(*Balaenoptera musculus*)
length 29.5 m (97 ft)

© 2010 Encyclopædia Britannica, Inc.

She for a long time she has been happy swimming and knowing the depths of the Antarctic, from where she has learned everything she knows.

She enjoys every day what the seabed that serves as her home offers her, the sea is hers, her world and there she feels like owner and mistress.

She is very selective and chooses who to share with, in that she is very similar to us. Every time she wants, she rises to the surface and that is why she knows the infinite sky. She there far away when she seems that the sea is over and she is confused with him, it is where she best feels herself and nothing without worrying.

When she feels like it, she goes down at depths crossing with other creatures that respect and love her.

Alba is very fast, which has saved her many times, but that time when she was swimming confidently, she has come to an end for her. The men made large, modern whalers and the catch of the whales moved to the Antarctic. Alba has never been able to sleep peacefully again. Her fleets chase her incessantly, they use all kinds of devices that discover her wherever she wants her to hide with her radars and they even shoot her from the air with her weapons flying in helicopters. If they knew Alba and could listen to her, they would not do these things, even some of her behaviors are very common in us humans. We should learn from these huge creatures and take advantage of her goodness to get to know them better and protect them.

The vastness of the ocean is infinite and its inhabitants existed long before man thought of populating the earth. Humans all together could get lost millions of times in the sea and be found by creatures like her. His predecessors

Great-great-grandparents knew the seabed and traveled great distances. Alba and her family have seen more than we have and they keep unheard of secrets that we should share. She only wants respect; she is willing to know us and our selfishness and ignorance does not leave us time to understand her.

The blue whale I know likes to be called Alba, she has told me many times when the dream wakes her up, in her exemplary goodness she has taken the first step with incredible sounds and vibrations that we do not try to hear, from her long conversations I have learned that you need to reclaim your space.

Alba, like us, wants to have a family and she needs her freedom, she has taught me that we can all live in peace, together strong and weak. She convinced me and I believed her, she has given us a vote of confidence. We can try, there is still time. Taking care of her we will be better and with our efforts we will also make our children know her one day.

Section 5

 **Learn and know the environment in which we live.**

Hydrological Cycle:

It is the process that describes the location and movement of water on our planet, in this continuous and irregular process in space and in time a particle of water evaporated from the ocean returns to the ocean after passing through different states or phases.

The hydrological cycle is defined as the sequence of permanent movement or transfer of water masses, both from one point of the planet to another, and between its different states (liquid, gas and solid). In this, the water passes from the earth's surface, in the vapor phase, to the atmosphere and returns in its liquid and solid phases.

The transfer of water from the Earth's surface to the atmosphere, in the form of water vapor, is due to direct **evaporation**, **transpiration** by plants and animals, and by **sublimation** (direct passage from solid water to water vapor). This flow of water is produced by two main causes: Solar energy and gravity.

A raindrop can go through the whole cycle or part of it. The hydrological cycle not only transfers water vapor from the

Earth's surface to the atmosphere, but helps to keep the Earth's surface cooler and the atmosphere warmer. In addition, it plays a vital role, it allows to soften the temperatures and rainfall in different areas of the planet, exchanging heat and humidity between points that are sometimes very far away.

Solar energy is the source of thermal energy necessary for the passage of water from the liquid and solid phases to the vapor phase, and it is also the origin of the atmospheric circulations that transport water vapor and move clouds.

The force of gravity causes precipitation and runoff. The hydrological cycle is a modeling agent of the earth's crust due to erosion and the transport and deposition of sediments by hydraulic means. It conditions the vegetation cover and, more generally, life on Earth.

The heating of tropical regions due to solar radiation causes the continuous evaporation of water from the oceans, which is transported in the form of water vapor by the general circulation of the atmosphere, to other regions. During transfer, part of the water vapor condenses due to cooling and forms clouds that cause precipitation.

Water vapor is transported by atmospheric circulation and condenses after having traveled distances that can exceed 1,000 km. The condensed water gives rise to the formation of fogs and clouds and, later, to precipitation.

Precipitation can occur in the liquid phase (rain) or in the solid phase (snow or hail). The water precipitated in the solid phase has a crystalline structure, in the case of snow, and a granular structure, regular in layers, in the case of hail.

Precipitation also includes water that passes from the atmosphere to the earth's surface by condensation of water vapor (dew) or by freezing of vapor (from water droplets in mists (clouds that touch the ground or the sea).

Simplified diagram of the Hydrological cycle.

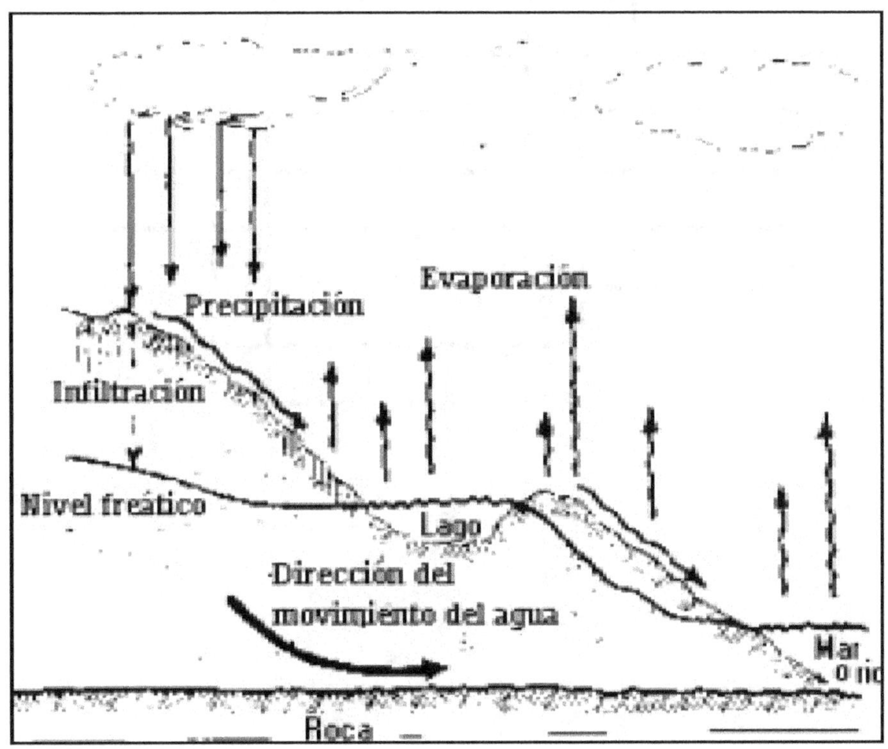

Section 6. Crossword "Natural"

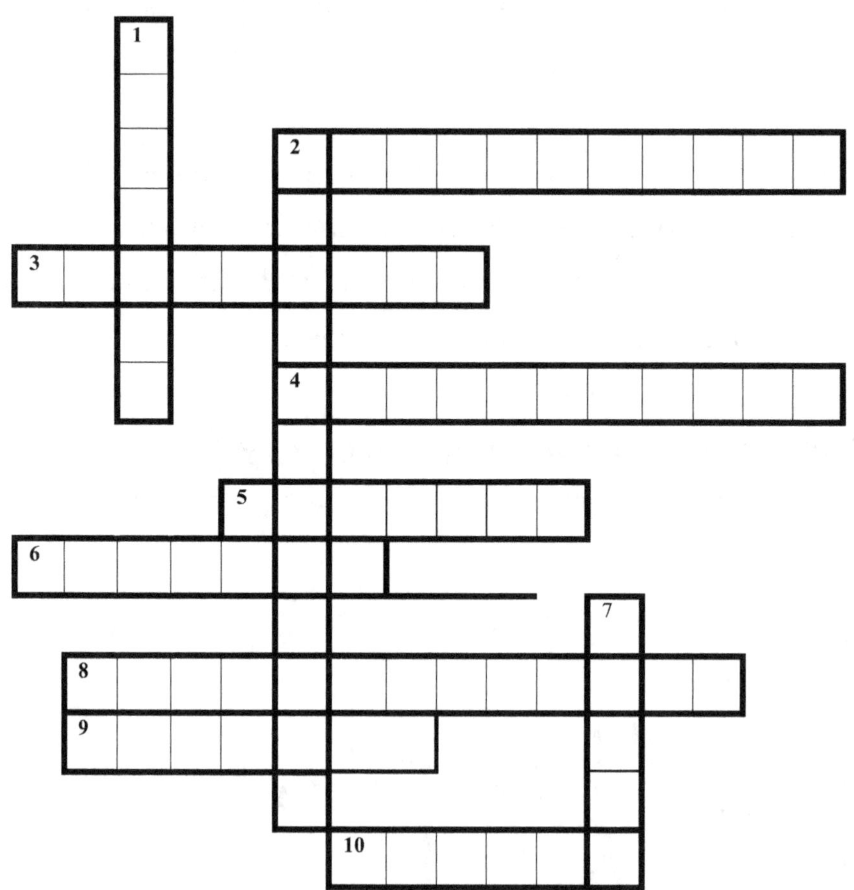

<u>**Vertical**</u> (from left to right).

(1) It is the permanent accumulation of ice in places where the volume of solid precipitation (snow) exceeds the volume of meltwater.

(2) Cyclical process of water in which it changes from a gaseous to a liquid state.

(7) Masses of frozen water that maintain a very low temperature.

<u>**Horizontal**</u> (from top to bottom).

(2) Natural phenomena or not, which occur in nature and cause damage to living beings.

(3) Center of any natural catastrophe.

(4) A continuous natural phenomenon that occurs in the seas when the atmospheric temperature is high.

(5) Waves that form in the sea of great energy.

(6)) Names of phenomena occurring in nature.

(8) Name used to refer to the fall of water to earth in the form of rain.

(9) Extremely strong wind produced by a small and very abrupt atmospheric depression that moves in large circles around itself and originates in tropical areas.

(10) Large bodies of water containing salts of (NaCl) Sodium chloride.

Section 7. Vocabulary and Concepts to consolidate.

When a body, due to the action of heat or cold, passes from one state to another, we say that it has changed state. In the case of water: when it is hot, ice melts and if we heat liquid water it evaporates. In addition to temperature, pressure also influences the state of substances.

When heating a solid, there comes a time when it turns into a liquid. This process is called **fusion**.

The **fusion point** is the temperature that a solid substance must reach to melt. Every substance has a characteristic fusion point. For example, the melting point of pure water is 0 ° Centigrade at normal atmospheric pressure.

When you heat a liquid, it turns into a gas. This process is called **vaporization**.

When vaporization takes place throughout the mass of liquid, forming bubbles of vapor inside it, it is called **boiling**. Also, the boiling temperature is characteristic of each substance and is called the boiling point. The **boiling point** of water is 100 °C at normal atmospheric pressure.

Transpiration: It is the phenomenon that occurs in the plant when the water absorbed by the roots reaches the upper parts of the plant and in the leaves through the stomata of the leaves due to the combined effect of factors such as temperature, winds and atmospheric pressure and it can enter the atmosphere again.

Japanese **tsunami** literally (great wave in the port) or tidal wave is a wave or a group of waves of great energy that occurs when some extraordinary phenomenon vertically displaces a large body of water. It is estimated that 90% of them are caused by earthquakes, in which case they are called tectonic tsunamis.

Epicenter: It is the point on the surface of the earth that corresponds to the vertical of the earthquake's focus, this point is the most devastated by this natural phenomenon. The center of any other major natural disaster is also called the epicenter.

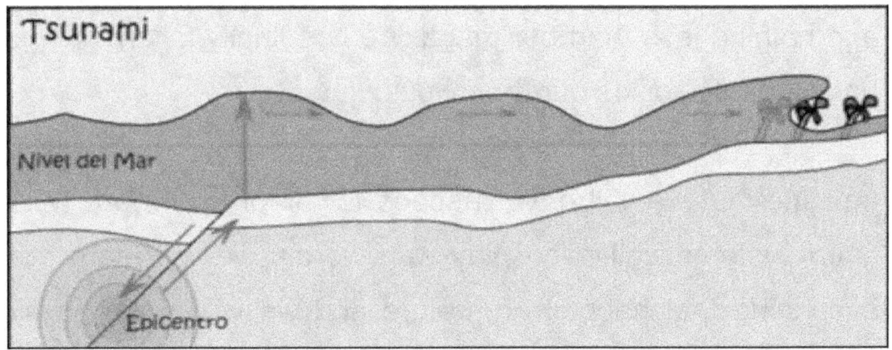

Section 8. Get updated.

-Get update. On June 26, it was 13 years and six months since the tsunami hit Southeast Asia. In the Kanyakumari district, where the Medicus -mundi project is located, there were 70,000 affected people who were taken in in 78 camps covering 31 villages. The schools became host camps. They help people temporarily. They have been provided with food, clothing, medicine, etc. Psychological support is also provided, as many of them are suffering the aftermath of the disaster.

Have you heard of the belt of fire? ... No? get update.

-The fire belt is the area most affected by Tsunamis, it is located in the Pacific Ocean and it is called that because it is the most active area on the planet.

-¡Listennnnnnnnn! Aqüitín has new news for you. Nothing more and nothing less than our magazine has finally fallen into good hands, fertile soil as our drop would say.

Imagine that we will have a space for all of us, where we will learn systematically and play with words, we will learn about everything that happens in nature and we will make possible with our knowledge a better future for tomorrow, in which the earth will be the home of all of us who know how to love the most. The children.

-Last news from the world of water business, imagine that the multinationals Danone, Nestlé and Coca-Cola control a good part of the water business. The privileged and great bottled water business.

The recent news about the scandal of the sale of tap water (apparently purified and enriched) by Coca-Cola in the UK are the tip of the iceberg behind the bottled water business.

The background is not restricted to more deception of the consumer about the type and quality of water that he is buying, but covers a series of aspects about a business that is sustained by the privatization of a vital and public resource. It is a business that is sustained by the sale of a vital and public resource that rarely pays for its private marketing.

The multinationals in the business appropriate the water from the countries where they are established. Thus, Danone, Nestlé or Coca-Cola are doing the bulk of their business with liquid from foreign countries, and to a much lesser extent with their own water (see attached table). This translates, depending on the legislation of each country, in which the water with which multinationals do business, goes from being a property of the Nation to a private property.

From our magazine we express our disagreement. Aqüitín, together with the Children's Water School, repudiates events like these, in which millions of people will be victims of these negotiations, including children who are always the most vulnerable.

Section 9 Announcements.

Haven't you Heard about our contest yet? You are on time. Prepare your drawing, story or poetry.

T *Aqüitin invites all schools and institutes*

The First International competition. of Drawing, Story and Poetry "A BETTER WORLD IS POSSIBLE". In tribute to World Water Day that is March 22 and World Environment Day that is celebrated on June 5.

¡¡Participate and Join our AQÜITÍN team!!

The works will be received from the current date until June 5, 2021 Environment Day, the last day to send them.

<u>General Rules of the Contest:</u>

All works in any of the three categories will be sent online to the email address albaortizmayo2008@yahoo.es
Drawing.

The drawings will be made on cardboard or paper that does not exceed 20x20 cm. And that they will send scans in (jpg) format

They will be able to participate by dividing themselves into three age groups.

Children 6-8 years.
9-11 years.
12-14 years.

Categories Poetry and Stories

Children 7-11 years.

12-14 years.

The works will be presented in (Word) format typed at 1.5 spaces. Letter Time New Roman 12 or if you prefer in his own handwriting with a ballpoint pen and legibly written all in capital letters. Do not exceed a maximum of two pages for poetry and four pages for stories.

They will be able to participate in the three category activities at the same time, sending the general data separately.

All MAIL SHIPMENTS must have TWO ATTACHMENTS, ONE WITH THE WORK AND ANOTHER FILE WITH THE DATA in the escrow (Name, age, home address, telephone number, School and school level).

In the subject of the email you will put **AQÜITÍN**

(International Drawing, Short Story and Poetry "A BETTER WORLD IS POSSIBLE")

The awards in the three categories will be made by age groups: three prizes for poetry and three for stories for each age group and the same for Drawing in its two age groups.

The awarded works will be published in the edition of the Magazine CORRESPONDING TO THE month of July **with the recognition of WINNERS of the competition in this FIRST INTERNATIONAL CONTEST**

<u>**For more information:**</u>

Contact the magazine's management at
E-mail (albaortizmayo2008@yahoo.es)

Natural crossword answers

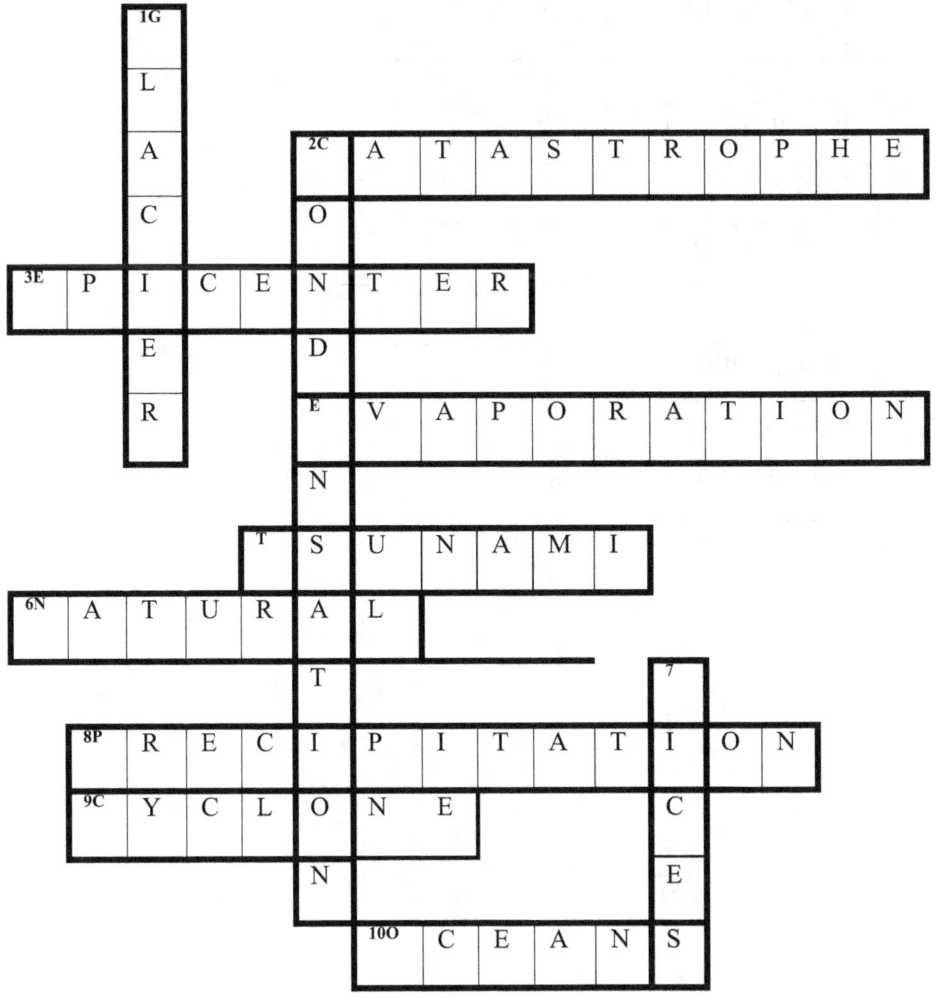

HORIZONTAL	VERTICAL
Catástrophe (2)	Glacier (1)
Epicenter (3)	Condensation (2)
Evaporation (4)	Ices (7)
Tsunami (5)	
Natural (6)	
Precipitation (8)	
Cyclone (9)	
Oceans (10)	

BIBLIOGRAPHY

- National Geographic News.

- Nature, at the service of water - Aquae Foundation

- www.fundacionaquae.org

Translaters:

Lic José M. Ramos Hernández
Graduated at the University
in Education Biology. Researcher Writer of
Literacy of Divulgation Scientific. Member
of the Society Speleology and Zoology
from Cuba and Dragonfly Society of the
Americas (DSA), USA The Bat Conservation
International (BCI), USA.

Lic Yolanda F. Rodríguez Toledo
Degree in Sociocultutal Studies Writer and
Poet Prestigious. Esp. Integrated Management
System and Quality Management
Metrology and Standarization